Pupil Book 3B

D1727586

Series Editor: Peter Clarke

Authors: Elizabeth Jurgensen, Jeanette Mumford, Sandra Roberts

Contents

3-digit numbers

Recognise the place value of each digit in a 3-digit number

Challenge 1

1 Write the numbers shown by the Base 10.

You will need:
- Base 10 blocks

2 Use your own Base 10 to make the numbers below.

a 126   b 164   c 119   d 237   e 242   f 266

Challenge 2

1 Write the numbers shown by the Base 10.

2 Write the numbers that have been separated into 100s, 10s and 1s.

| a | 200 | 10 | 9 | b | 400 | 50 | 5 | c | 500 | 70 | 9 |
| d | 600 | 20 | 9 | e | 700 | 70 | 3 | f | 800 | 0 | 8 |

Challenge 3

1 Write the numbers that have been separated into 100s, 10s and 1s.

| a | 80 | 500 | 3 | b | 4 | 800 | 30 | c | 10 | 500 | 1 |
| d | 900 | 9 | 30 | e | 70 | 800 | 4 | f | 80 | 700 | 6 |

2 I'm thinking of a number. The 100s digit is between 4 and 6, the 10s digit is 7 and the 1s digit is an odd number. Write as many possible answers as you can.

Ordering numbers to 1000

Compare and order numbers up to 1000

Challenge 1

Order each set of numbers, smallest to largest.

a (254, 168, 517, 429) b 572, 266, 103, 381 c 467, 236, 423, 351

d (109, 541, 377, 218) e 276, 317, 180, 441 f 288, 371, 125, 452

g 151, 132, 169, 124 h 183, 137, 142, 193 i 258, 231, 227, 263

j 238, 254, 286, 207 k 283, 253, 213, 243 l 376, 384, 362, 390

Challenge 2

1 Order each set of numbers, smallest to largest.

a 265, 832, 163, 589, 322   b 831, 538, 529, 187, 276

c 945, 276, 254, 723, 433   d 376, 512, 352, 589, 312

e 478, 492, 382, 319, 408   f 821, 903, 962, 855, 965

g 444, 402, 414, 490, 476   h 899, 843, 856, 809, 819

2 For each number, write a 3-digit number that is larger and one that is smaller.

a 457 / 456 / 455   b 379 / 378 / 377   c 246 / 245 / 244   d 891 / 890 / 889

e 800 / 799 / S:798   f 802 / 801 / S:801   g 922 / 921 / S:920   h 944 / 943 / 942

Challenge 3

1 Write a set of instructions for ordering 3-digit numbers.

2 Using the cards, make two 3-digit numbers that are larger than the number on each of the whiteboards above.

2 5 8 9

Using money to show 3-digit numbers

Represent and estimate numbers using money

Challenge 1

What amounts are shown here? Write each answer as cents.

a   10c 10c 10c 1c 1c 1c 1c

b   10c 10c 10c 10c 1c 1c 1c

Example

€1 + 10c + 10c + 10c + 10c + 1c = 141c

c   10c 10c 10c 10c 10c 1c

d   10c 10c 1c 1c 1c 1c 1c

e   10c 10c 10c 10c 1c 1c 1c 1c 1c 1c 1c

f   €1 10c 10c 1c 1c 1c   g   €1 10c 10c 10c 1c 1c 1c

h   €1 €1 10c 10c 10c 1c   i   €1 €1 10c 10c 1c 1c 1c 1c 1c 1c 1c

Challenge 2

1   What amounts are shown here? Write each answer as cents.

a   €1 €1 10c 10c 10c 1c 1c 1c

b   €1 €1 10c 10c 10c 10c 1c 1c 1c 1c 1c

Example

€1 + €1 + 10c + 10c + 1c = 221c

c   €1 €1 €1 10c 10c 1c 1c 1c 1c

d   €1 €1 €1 €1 10c 10c 10c 10c 1c 1c

e   €1 €1 €1 €1 €1 10c 10c 10c 10c 10c

f   €1 €1 €1 €1 €1 €1 10c 1c 1c 1c

2   What coins would you need to make these amounts?

a   245c   b   316c   c   453c   d   507c   e   732c   f   663c

Challenge 3

Imagine you had 8 coins in your pocket –
they could be €1 coins, 10c coins or 1c coins.
What amount of money might you have?
Find different amounts.

Example

€1 + €1 + €1
+ 10c + 10c + 10c
+ 1c + 1c = 332c

Get the order

Compare and order numbers up to 1000

Work in threes.

- One player secretly writes a number on each of the pieces of paper.
- The other two players write the numbers 1–6 as a list in their books. At the top of the page, write: 'largest' and at the bottom write: 'smallest'.
- The player with the numbers reads them out one at a time.
- The other players decide where to write the number on their list.
- Players keep going until all the numbers have been read out.
- If a number cannot be put in order, write it next to the list.

Challenge 1

1 Secretly write a 2-digit number on each of the six pieces of paper.

2 How many of the numbers are in order?

3 Play again, this time with a different player writing the six secret numbers.

You will need:
- six small pieces of paper

Challenge 2

1 Secretly write a 3-digit number on each of the six pieces of paper.

2 Explain how you made your choices about where to write the numbers.

3 How can you improve your ordering next time?

You will need:
- six small pieces of paper

Challenge 3

1 Secretly write a 3-digit number on each of the ten pieces of paper. The other players write the numbers 1–10 as a list.

2 Which numbers did you find hardest to order? Explain why.

3 Write three top tips for playing this game. Try them out in the next round.

You will need:
- ten small pieces of paper

Café totals

Add amounts of money

How much would it cost to buy these items from the café?

Challenge 1

a apple juice and fairy cake

b orange juice and banana

c sausage roll and apple juice

d cheese sandwich and banana

e orange juice and fairy cake

f sausage roll and banana

apple juice 34c

orange juice 37c

cheese sandwich 58c

sausage roll 45c

fairy cake 42c

banana 25c

Challenge 2

a cup of tea and tuna sandwich

b ice cream and cheese toastie

c apple pie and cup of tea

d tuna sandwich and apple pie

e ice cream and cheese toastie

f apple pie and ice cream

apple pie 50c

cheese toastie 80c

ice cream 72c

tuna sandwich 74c

cup of tea 65c

Challenge 3

1 a egg sandwich and mango juice

b cheese toastie and milkshake

c hot chocolate and egg sandwich

d carrot cake and mango juice

e egg sandwich and cheese toastie

f milkshake and carrot cake

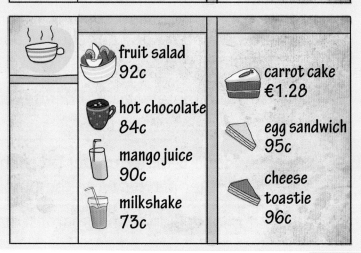

fruit salad 92c

hot chocolate 84c

mango juice 90c

milkshake 73c

carrot cake €1.28

egg sandwich 95c

cheese toastie 96c

2 I bought three things in the café. I spent a total of €2.96. What did I buy?

Café change

Subtract amounts of money to give change

mini pizza 84c
ice cream 72c
cup of tea 65c
milkshake 73c

carrot cake €1.28
cheese toastie 96c
slice of toast 21c

apple juice 34c
orange juice 37c
tuna sandwich 74c
sausage roll 45c

fairy cake 42c
banana 25c
fruit salad 92c
hot chocolate 84c

Challenge 1

Daniel has 50c. How much change will he get if he buys these things at the café?

   a   apple juice   b   banana   c   fairy cake

   d   slice of toast   e   sausage roll   f   orange juice

Challenge 2

1 Youssef has €1 (100c). How much change will he get if he buys these things?

   a   fairy cake   b   cup of tea   c   mini pizza

   d   ice cream   e   tuna sandwich   f   apple juice

2 Explain how to find change.

Challenge 3

1 Irene has €2 (200c). How much change will she get if she buys these things?

   a   fruit salad   b   orange juice   c   cheese toastie

   d   hot chocolate   e   carrot cake   f   milkshake

2 How much change will Sam get from €2 (200c) if she buys these things?

   a   orange juice and carrot cake   b   hot chocolate and cheese toastie

   c   milkshake and fruit salad

Buying fruit

Add and subtract amounts of money

Challenge 1

You have €1 (100c). How much change will you get if you buy this fruit?

a 1 orange	b 100 g of grapes	c 1 apple
d 100 g of plums	e 1 apple and 1 orange	f 2 pears
g 1 pear and 1 orange	h 2 apples	i 2 oranges

Challenge 2

You have €2 (200c). How much change will you get if you buy this fruit?

a 1 melon	b 100 g of strawberries
c 1 orange and 1 apple	d 200 g of grapes
e 100 g of plums and a pear	f 200 g of bananas
g 1 melon and 1 orange	h 100 g of strawberries and 100 g of grapes

Challenge 3

You have €5 (500c). How much change will you get if you buy this fruit?

a 200 g of strawberries	b 1 melon and 1 orange
c 100 g of strawberries and 100 g of plums	d 2 melons
e 1 apple and 100 g of bananas	f 200 g of plums
g 3 apples	h 300 g of grapes

Furniture shopping

- Add and subtract amounts of money
- Solve word problems involving money and reason mathematically

Mina, Lily and Jacob are buying new items for their bedrooms. Mina has €100, Jacob has €200 and Lily has €500 to spend.

Work out these money problems. Show your working out.

Challenge 1

a Jacob buys a rug and a mirror. How much does he spend?

b Lily chooses the most expensive item in the shop. How much does it cost?

c Mina buys a desk. How much change will she get?

d Lily buys a desk and a rug. How much do they cost?

Challenge 2

a Mina wants a bookcase and a mirror. How much more money does she need?

b Lily buys the two most expensive items. What will the total be?

c Jacob chooses the cheapest item in the shop. How much change will he get?

d Lily buys a rug, mirror and a desk. How much will she spend?

Challenge 3

a Lily buys a bed and a mirror. How much change does she get?

b Mina wants a bookcase and a wardrobe. How much more money does she need?

c Jacob buys two rugs and a mirror. How much change will he get?

d If Mina and Jacob put their money together, can they buy 3 armchairs?

Drawing and naming shapes

Draw and name 2-D shapes

You will need:
- Resource 21:
  3 x 3 pinboards
- ruler

 Challenge 1

1 Name these shapes.

A   B   C   D   E   F   G   H

2 Using Resource 21: 3 x 3 pinboards, draw these shapes.

    a triangle b square c rectangle d pentagon e hexagon

 Challenge 2

1 Name these shapes.

You will need:
- ruler
- squared paper

A   B   C   D   E   F

2 Draw these shapes on squared paper.

    a a square with sides of 4 cm   b a rectangle with sides of 3 cm and 4 cm

    c 2 different pentagons   d 2 different hexagons

 Challenge 3

Using Resource 21: 3 x 3 pinboards, draw ten different 4-sided shapes.

You will need:
- Resource 21: 3 x 3 pinboards
- ruler

Matching 2-D shapes

Make shapes that match a property

You will need:
• Resource 22:
  Matching shapes (1)
• scissors
• squared paper
• ruler
• blue and red pencils

Challenge 1

1 Using Resource 22: Matching shapes (1), join two triangles along matching edges to make these shapes.

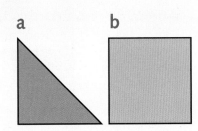

2 a Draw the two shapes above on squared paper.

   b Rule a blue line to show how the triangles fit together.

   c Circle the right angles in red.

Challenge 2

Work with a partner.

a Cut out the rectangle and two triangles on Resource 24: Matching shapes (2).

b Make the shapes below using the rectangle and the right-angled triangles.

c Draw each shape showing how you made it using the rectangle and triangles.

You will need:
• Resource 24:
  Matching shapes (2)
• scissors
• squared paper
• ruler

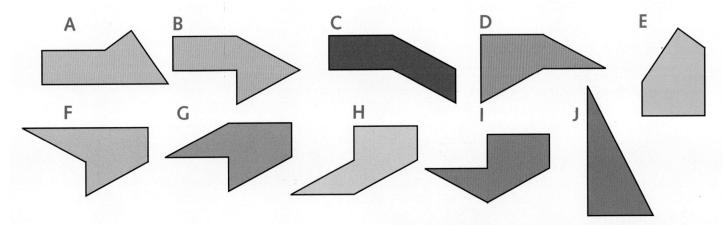

A   B   C   D   E

F   G   H   I   J

Challenge 3

Look at the ten shapes in Challenge 2. Copy and complete the table.

Property	Shape
has one right angle	
has more than one right angle	A,

13

Paper shapes

Make shapes using folding and cutting

You will need:
- paper squares or circles
- scissors
- ruler
- pen
- glue

 Challenge 1

1 Fold the paper square into quarters.

2 Make these patterns by folding and cutting. Mark the lines of symmetry with a pen. Stick the patterns in your book.

a   b   c

Challenge 2

1 Fold the paper circle and squares into quarters.

2 Find ways to make these patterns. Mark the lines of symmetry with a pen. Stick the patterns in your book.

Challenge 3

Design two more patterns of your own. Mark any lines of symmetry and stick them in your exercise book.

Properties of 2-D shapes

Describe the properties of 2-D shapes

 Challenge 1

Read the clues. Find the shape. Write its name.

a I have 5 equal sides.

b I have 1 right angle and 3 sides.

c I have equal sides and 4 right angles.

d I have 6 equal angles all greater than a right angle.

 Challenge 2

1 Take two triangles and one regular shape from Resource 61: 2-D shapes. Fit them together to make these shapes. Name each shape.

You will need:
• Resource 61: 2-D shapes
• right-angle tester
• ruler
• scissors

A   B   C   D   E

2 Solve these puzzles about the shapes in Question 1.

a I have 2 angles greater than a right angle and 2 angles less than a right angle. Which shape am I?

b I have 1 right angle and my 6 sides are equal in length. Which shape am I?

 Challenge 3

Andy said, "I can use 12 rods to make 5 squares." Is he correct? Sketch the squares you make.

You will need:
• Twelve 10 rods from Base 10 materials

Counting in steps of 2, 4 and 8

Count in multiples of 2, 4 and 8

 Write the missing numbers.

a   2, 4, ____ , 8, ____ , ____ , ____ , ____ , 18, ____ , ____ , 24

b   4, ____ , ____ ,16 , ____ , ____ , ____ , ____ , 36, ____ , 44 ____

c   8, ____ , 24, ____ , ____ , ____ , 56, ____ , ____ , ____ , 88

1 Find the multiples of each number and write them in order, smallest to largest.

a multiples of 2

21   2   18
6   4   14
9   10   13

b multiples of 4

32   12   36
4   34   16
22   20   18

c multiples of 8

8   72   48
36   24   45
56   52   32

2 Add the numbers to find the total.

a   2 + 4 + 4 = ____

b   2 + 4 + 8 = ____

c   4 + 4 + 8 = ____

d   8 + 8 + 4 + 4 = ____

e   2 + 8 + 8 + 2 + 8 + 2 = ____

f   4 + 4 + 8 + 8 + 2 + 8 + 4 = ____

Read each clue to find the number.

a   We are multiples of 2, 4 and 8. We are between 20 and 50.

b   I am a multiple of 2, 4 and 8. I am less than 40. I have a 3 in the 10s place.

c   I am a multiple of 2, 4 and 8. I am also a multiple of 3. I am less than 40.

Halving to find the division facts for the 4 multiplication table

Use halving to recall the division facts for the 4 multiplication table

Challenge 1

Write the number that is half of each of these numbers.

a 24   b 46   c 38   d 64   e 88   f 16

g 36   h 18   i 62   j 32   k 48   l 44

Challenge 2

Divide each array by 4. Use the halve and halve again strategy to work out each answer. Write the division calculations for each array.

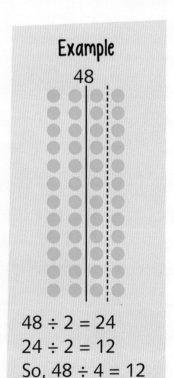

Example
48

$48 \div 2 = 24$
$24 \div 2 = 12$
So, $48 \div 4 = 12$

Challenge 3

Answer these division facts about 4 using the halve and halve again strategy. Show your working.

a $60 \div 4 =$ ☐

b $72 \div 4 =$ ☐

c $64 \div 4 =$ ☐

d $56 \div 4 =$ ☐

e $76 \div 4 =$ ☐

f $92 \div 4 =$ ☐

Halving to find the division facts for the 8 multiplication table

Use halving to recall the division facts for the 8 multiplication table

Challenge 1

Write the number that is half of these numbers, then halve the number again.

a 16   b 48   c 24   d 40   e 12

f 32   g 20   h 36   i 28   j 80

Challenge 2

Divide each array of chocolate bars by 8. Use the halve, halve again and then halve again strategy to work out each answer. Write the division calculations for each array.

Example

40

$40 \div 2 = 20$
$20 \div 2 = 10$
$10 \div 2 = 5$
So, $40 \div 8 = 5$

a 16   b 80   c 24   d 88   e 32   f 56   g 48

Challenge 3

Answer these division facts about 8. Halve each number three times to find the answer. Show your working.

a $112 \div 8 =$ ☐   b $128 \div 8 =$ ☐

c $104 \div 8 =$ ☐   d $120 \div 8 =$ ☐

e $144 \div 8 =$ ☐   f $168 \div 8 =$ ☐

Solving word problems (5)

Solve word problems and reason mathematically

Challenge 1

Write the answers to these number facts.

a 4 x 8   b 6 x 4   c 64 ÷ 8   d 36 ÷ 3

e 9 x 4   f 72 ÷ 8   g 27 ÷ 3   h 9 x 8   i 56 ÷ 8

Challenge 2

Look at the drinks for sale.
Read each question below.
Decide which operation to use.
Write the calculation, then write
the answer to the problem.

a Matt buys 7 single cups of juice.
How much does he pay?

b Jim buys three 4-cup trays of juice
and 1 single cup of juice. How many
cups has he bought altogether?

c Fran buys one 8-cup tray of juice.
How much does each cup cost?

d Mary buys two 8-cup trays of juice
and 3 single cups of juice. How
much does she pay?

e Jake wants to buy 25 cups of juice.
He has €50. Does he have enough
money? Explain your answer.

f Is it better to buy four 2-cup trays
of juice or one 8-cup tray of juice?
Why?

Challenge 3

Use the pictures above to make up your own word problems with the
calculations below.

a 6 x 8 =   b 72 ÷ 8 = ⬤   c (4 x 3) + (1 x 3) = ◯

d 7 x ⬤ = 28   e (6 x 2) + (3 x 8) =

Fractions and division

Recognise, find and write unit fractions of a set of objects

Challenge 1

Find half of each set of stamps.

a b c d

e f g

Example

$\frac{1}{2}$ of 6 = 3

Challenge 2

1 Find half of these numbers. Write your answer as a division calculation and as a fraction calculation.

a 14　　b 18　　c 24　　d 28　　e 34

f 36　　g 40　　h 46　　i 42　　j 54

Example

$12 \div 2 = 6$

$\frac{1}{2}$ of 12 = 6

2 Find a quarter of these numbers. Write your answer as a division calculation and as a fraction calculation.

a 12　　b 20　　c 24　　d 32　　e 40　　f 48

Example

$12 \div 4 = 3$

$\frac{1}{4}$ of 12 = 3

3 Find a third of these numbers. Write your answer as a division calculation and as a fraction calculation.

a 18　　b 27　　c 36　　d 21　　e 42　　f 48

Example

$24 \div 3 = 8$

$\frac{1}{3}$ of 24 = 8

4 Explain how you know what to divide by to find a fraction of any number.

Challenge 3

1 What fractions of each of these numbers can you find? Write all the possibilities. Write your answers as a division calculation and as a fraction calculation.

a 15　　b 20　　c 24　　d 27　　e 32　　f 40

2 Write three top tips for finding fractions of numbers.

Fraction snakes

Investigate non-unit fractions

You will need:
- coloured pencils
- squared paper

Challenge 1

1 Look at these snakes. Write the fractions that describe each snake.

Example

$\frac{1}{6}$ blue and $\frac{5}{6}$ yellow

2 Draw your own snakes 7 squares long. Colour them in using 2 different colours. Write the fractions that describe each snake.

Challenge 2

1 Look at these snakes. Write the fractions that describe each snake.

2 Draw snakes 10 squares long. A snake 10 squares long can be described using tenths and fifths. Colour the snakes in as many different ways as you can and write the fractions that describe each snake.

Challenge 3

1 Take a handful of cubes in two different colours and use them to make a snake. Draw the snake. Write the fractions.

You will need:
- 20 interlocking cubes

2 Take a handful of cubes in three different colours and use them to make a snake. Draw the snake. Write the fractions.

Ordering fractions

Compare and order unit fractions and fractions with the same denominator

 Challenge 1   Write the fraction that describes the coloured part of each circle.

1 a ⊘ **b** ⊘ **c** ⊘ **d** ⊘   **2 a** ⊘ **b** ⊘ **c** ⊘ **d** ⊘

3 a ⊘ **b** ⊘ **c** ⊘ **d** ⊘   **4 a** ⊘ **b** ⊘ **c** ⊘ **d** ⊘

5 Now put each set of fractions in order, smallest to largest.

 Challenge 2   **1** Order each set of fractions, smallest to largest.

a	$\frac{3}{4}$	$\frac{1}{4}$	$\frac{2}{4}$	$\frac{4}{4}$	**b**	$\frac{3}{8}$	$\frac{6}{8}$	$\frac{1}{8}$	$\frac{2}{8}$
c	$\frac{4}{9}$	$\frac{8}{9}$	$\frac{2}{9}$	$\frac{5}{9}$	**d**	$\frac{4}{6}$	$\frac{2}{6}$	$\frac{5}{6}$	$\frac{6}{6}$

2 Write instructions for ordering fractions when the denominators are all the same.

3 Would you rather have $\frac{2}{8}$ or $\frac{5}{8}$ of a chocolate cake? Explain why.

Challenge 3   **1** Order each set of fractions, smallest to largest.

a	$\frac{1}{4}$	$\frac{1}{2}$	$\frac{1}{10}$	$\frac{1}{5}$	**b**	$\frac{1}{6}$	$\frac{1}{7}$	$\frac{1}{2}$	$\frac{1}{3}$
c	$\frac{1}{9}$	$\frac{1}{4}$	$\frac{1}{6}$	$\frac{1}{12}$	**d**	$\frac{1}{17}$	$\frac{1}{3}$	$\frac{1}{5}$	$\frac{1}{11}$

2 Write instructions for ordering fractions with different denominators.

3 What does the denominator tell us about the fraction?

Fractions on number lines

Write fractions on number lines

Write the missing fractions on these number lines.

a 0   1

b 0 $\frac{2}{4}$ 1

c 0 $\frac{1}{5}$ $\frac{4}{5}$ 1

d 0 $\frac{2}{6}$ 1

e 0 $\frac{3}{7}$ $\frac{5}{7}$ 1

f 0 $\frac{1}{8}$ $\frac{4}{8}$ 1

1 Complete these fraction number lines.

a quarters   0 _____ 1   b thirds   0 _____ 1

c fifths   0 _____ 1

d eighths   0 _____ 1

2 Write the next four fractions after 1.

a $\frac{3}{4}$, 1,   ,   ,

b $\frac{4}{6}$, $\frac{5}{6}$, 1,   ,   ,

c $\frac{6}{8}$, $\frac{7}{8}$, 1,   ,   ,

d $\frac{2}{3}$, 1,   ,   ,

e $\frac{8}{10}$, $\frac{9}{10}$, 1,   ,   ,

f $\frac{7}{9}$, $\frac{8}{9}$, 1,   ,   ,

Draw two number lines and write these fractions on them.

a $\frac{1}{2}$, $\frac{1}{4}$, $\frac{3}{4}$, $\frac{1}{3}$, $\frac{2}{3}$

b $\frac{1}{2}$, $\frac{1}{4}$, $\frac{3}{4}$, $\frac{1}{8}$, $\frac{3}{8}$, $\frac{5}{8}$, $\frac{7}{8}$

Measuring in centimetres

Use a ruler to draw and measure lines to the nearest centimetre

You will need:
• ruler

A
B
C
D
E

1 Measure the length of each line to the nearest centimetre. Copy and complete the table.

Line	A	B	C	D	E
Length in cm					

2 Draw lines that are 5 cm longer than lines A and B.

3 Draw lines that are $2\frac{1}{2}$ cm shorter than lines C, D and E. Write the new length above the line.

Challenge 3

Henry said, "If I take a length of ribbon from each basket and sew them together, I can make 6 different lengths."

a Is he correct? Investigate.

b What is the longest length of ribbon he can make?

30 cm
50 cm
70 cm
7 cm
9 cm

Measuring in millimetres

Use a ruler to draw and measure lines to the nearest millimetre

You will need:
• ruler

 Challenge 1

1 Draw lines of these lengths.

    a 10 mm **b** 30 mm **c** 80 mm **d** 55 mm **e** 25 mm **f** 75 mm

2 Measure these objects to the nearest millimetre.

    a   **b**   **c**

Example

31 mm

Challenge 2

1 Measure each rod in millimetres, then draw a line of the same length. Below the line, write the length in two ways.

    a

    b

    c

    d

    e

Example

54 mm
= 5 cm 4 mm

2 Draw lines of these lengths:

    a 3 cm shorter than 85 mm   **b** 4 cm longer than 58 mm

Challenge 3

Amy needs 4 buttons of the same size. This is her collection of buttons. Which size of button does she choose?

Measuring and comparing lengths

Measure and compare lengths and multiples of lengths in m and cm

Challenge 1

Work with a partner.
Find pairs of objects.
For each pair:
- measure and compare their lengths
- find their total length

Example

21 cm   28 cm

Book B is 7 cm longer than Book A.
The total length is 49 cm.

You will need:
- ruler
- measuring tape
- collection of objects to measure

Challenge 2

1 Work with a partner. Place the objects on the floor. Estimate, then measure the distance between them in metres and centimetres. Do this five times and compare each measure with its estimate.

Example

Estimate: 3 m 10 cm

3 m 35 cm

Measure: 3 m 35 cm

2 Jim stacks boxes in a warehouse. He has a delivery of three sizes of boxes. Find the total height when he makes a stack of 2, 4, 5 and 10 of each box. Copy and complete the table.

	2 boxes	4 boxes	5 boxes	10 boxes
Box A				
Box B				
Box C				

Challenge 3

Work with a partner. Find the distance, in metres, between two objects in the playground, for example, width of front door, length of flowerbed, distance to gate. Your teacher will suggest suitable things to measure.

Adding and subtracting lengths

Add and subtract length using mixed units

Challenge 1

Jim had four bendy straws, each 15 cm long. He bent each straw to make two parts. He used centimetres and millimetres to measure the parts. Copy and complete his results.

a   9 cm +   cm = 15 cm

b $7\frac{1}{2}$ cm +   cm = 15 cm

c   4 cm 5 mm +   cm   mm = 15 cm

d   12 cm 5 mm +   cm   mm = 15 cm

Example

7 cm

8 cm

8 cm + 7 cm = 15 cm

Challenge 2

R

S

T

1   Work out the length of Trucks R and T.

2   All three trucks board a ferry to Ireland. They park behind each other nose to tail. What is their total length?

3   A van is half the length of Truck S. What is its length?

- Truck R is 2 m 30 cm shorter than Truck S

- Truck S is 8 m 40 cm

- Truck T is $\frac{1}{2}$ m longer than Truck S

Challenge 3

There are five trucks waiting to board the ferry. The scale shows the height of each truck. Which truck is:

a   18 cm taller than Truck C?

b   25 cm short of 5 m?

c   26 cm shorter than Truck A?

d   What is the difference in height between Trucks A and E?

510 ←—Truck A
500 ←—Truck B
490 ←—Truck C
480 ←—Truck D
←—Truck E
470
cm

27

Expanded addition

- Add 3-digit numbers using the expanded written method of column addition
- Estimate the answer to a calculation

Challenge 1

Use the expanded method to add these numbers together. Make sure you write out each calculation correctly.

a 53 + 25	b 41 + 37	c 64 + 23	d 136 + 143
e 165 + 131	f 238 + 160	g 216 + 283	h 306 + 292

Example

```
   215
 + 342
─────
     7
    50
   500
─────
   557
```

Challenge 2

1 Read each calculation and quickly write an estimate of the answer.

a 285 + 417	b 258 + 431	c 392 + 307
d 445 + 313	e 427 + 436	f 308 + 395
g 417 + 387	h 226 + 479	i 516 + 247

Example

371 + 328

300 plus 300 is 600, and the 10s and 1s are nearly 100, so my estimate is 700.

2 Use the expanded method to work out the calculations in Question 1. Make sure you write out the calculation correctly.

Challenge 3

1 Read each calculation and quickly write an estimate of the answer.

a 406 + 389	b 517 + 378	c 605 + 389	d 468 + 474
e 547 + 463	f 738 + 255	g 179 + 808	h 643 + 397

2 Use the expanded method to work out the calculations in Question 1.

3 A pupil has written out this calculation. Explain what needs to be changed in their working out.

```
   312
 + 437
─────
     9
     4
     7
─────
   749
```

Column addition (1)

- Add 3-digit numbers using the formal written method of column addition
- Estimate the answer to a calculation

Challenge 1

1   Use the expanded method to add these numbers together.

a	235 + 141	b	173 + 206	c	267 + 132
d	159 + 130	e	286 + 213	f	324 + 255

Example
```
  317
+ 361
----
    8
   70
  600
----
  678
```

2   Work out these using the formal method.

a	153 + 232	b	275 + 213	c	241 + 356
d	374 + 223	e	261 + 327	f	321 + 264

Example
```
  317
+ 361
----
  678
```

Challenge 2

1   Estimate the answers to these calculations.

a	345 + 351	b	273 + 416	c	368 + 321	d	438 + 361
e	508 + 381	f	472 + 326	g	581 + 217	h	483 + 416

2   Use the formal method to work out the calculations in Question 1.

3   Use the formal method to add these numbers.

a	326 + 347	b	259 + 435	c	415 + 319	d	536 + 248
e	447 + 344	f	539 + 353	g	263 + 518	h	366 + 326

Challenge 3

1   Estimate the answers to these calculations.

a	538 + 358	b	482 + 409	c	558 + 237	d	627 + 359
e	736 + 246	f	555 + 438	g	837 + 158	h	574 + 316

2   Explain how to estimate the answers to addition calculations.

3   Use the formal method to work out the calculations in Question 1.

29

Column addition (2)

- Add 3-digit numbers using the formal written method of column addition
- Estimate the answer to a calculation

Challenge 1

First estimate the answers to these calculations.
Then use the formal method to add the numbers.

a 153 + 146	b 137 + 151	c 264 + 125	
d 216 + 243	e 357 + 221	f 208 + 381	
g 362 + 316	h 427 + 342	i 415 + 363	
j 512 + 374	k 206 + 681	l 467 + 531	

Example

162
+ 237
399

Remember, always start with the 1s!

Challenge 2

First estimate the answers to these calculations.
Then use the formal method to add the numbers.

1 Carry the 1s:

a 264 + 327	b 339 + 346	c 325 + 437	d 529 + 338
e 417 + 467	f 574 + 318	g 356 + 529	h 608 + 388

2 Carry the 10s:

a 463 + 274	b 532 + 394	c 467 + 481	d 573 + 345
e 295 + 642	f 485 + 361	g 563 + 354	h 492 + 485

Challenge 3

1 First estimate the answers to these calculations.
Then use the formal method to add these numbers.

a 418 + 347	b 562 + 374	c 635 + 284	d 381 + 409
e 762 + 193	f 574 + 372	g 418 + 546	h 719 + 159

2 These calculations need the 1s and the 10s carried.

a 257 + 365	b 362 + 359	c 476 + 287	d 658 + 176

Mental addition

Add numbers mentally and use the inverse operation to check the answer

Challenge 1

Make up twelve addition calculations using these numbers.

I like to work the calculations out mentally.

I prefer to draw an empty number line to work them out.

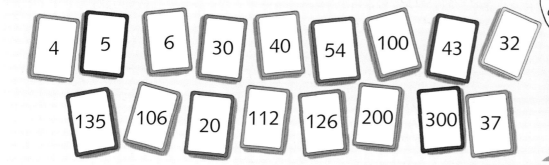

4 5 6 30 40 54 100 43 32

135 106 20 112 126 200 300 37

Challenge 2

1 Make up twelve addition calculations using these numbers.

6 7 8 50 60 70 76 69 72

81 328 387 563 400 500 600 465

2 Choose four of your calculations and use subtraction to check the answers.

Challenge 3

1 Make up twelve addition calculations using these numbers.

7 8 9 94 70 60 90 79 85

88 557 684 761 845 600 700 800

2 Choose two different calculations that you can do mentally. Explain what happens in your head when you work them out.

3 Choose four of your calculations and use subtraction to check the answers.

Column subtraction (1)

- Subtract 3-digit numbers using the formal written method of column subtraction
- Estimate the answer to a calculation

Challenge 1

Work out these calculations using the formal method.

a 37 – 14   b 58 – 45   c 49 – 26

d 63 – 31   e 275 – 131   f 264 – 142

g 285 – 151   h 297 – 165   i 235 – 124

j 265 – 143   k 379 – 156   l 368 – 234

Example

$$\begin{array}{r} 465 \\ -\ 213 \\ \hline 252 \end{array}$$

Challenge 2

1 First estimate the answers to these calculations.
Then work them out using the formal method.

a 457 – 236   b 483 – 251   c 548 – 313   d 577 – 241

e 476 – 124   f 596 – 371   g 485 – 223   h 536 – 204

2 In these calculations, you will need to change the 1s in the first number.

a 372 – 135   b 381 – 148   c 394 – 278   d 431 – 107

e 463 – 217   f 485 – 149   g 566 – 338   h 547 – 239

Challenge 3

1 Estimate the answers to the calculations below.

2 Explain how to estimate the answers to subtraction calculations.

3 Use the formal method to work out these calculations.

a 583 – 267   b 645 – 128   c 696 – 358   d 751 – 425

e 736 – 329   f 792 – 454   g 863 – 517   h 974 – 735

Column subtraction (2)

- Subtract 3-digit numbers using the formal written method of column subtraction
- Estimate the answer to a calculation

Challenge 1

First estimate the answers to these calculations.
Then use the formal method to subtract the numbers.

a 256 – 134	b 275 – 121	c 298 – 163
d 267 – 142	e 354 – 102	f 378 – 243
g 356 – 124	h 384 – 251	i 468 – 147

Example

478
– 353
125

Example

515
~~658~~
– 274
384

Challenge 2

First estimate the answers to these calculations.
Then use the formal method to subtract the numbers.

1 Change the 1s:

a 273 – 145	b 361 – 227	c 457 – 329	d 383 – 146

2 Change the 10s:

a 326 – 142	b 365 – 183	c 348 – 271	d 437 – 253
e 516 – 372	f 538 – 276	g 657 – 382	h 614 – 283

Challenge 3

1 First estimate the answers to these calculations.
   Then use the formal method to subtract these numbers.

a 439 – 256	b 518 – 353	c 654 – 217	d 582 – 355
e 464 – 231	f 627 – 156	g 758 – 429	h 708 – 341

2 These calculations need the 1s and the 10s changed. Work with a partner.

a 432 – 156	b 547 – 268	c 642 – 374	d 675 – 297
e 773 – 212	f 857 – 479	g 863 – 584	h 815 – 639

33

Mental subtraction

Subtract numbers mentally and use the inverse operation to check the answer

Challenge 1

Make up twelve subtraction calculations using these numbers.

I like to work the calculations out mentally.

I prefer to draw an empty number line to work them out.

65 - 7
427 - 8
361 - 40
542 - 300

4   6   6   20   30   40   47   41   54

59   167   152   148   163   100   200   300

Challenge 2

1 Make up twelve subtraction calculations using these numbers.

6   7   8   50   60   74   65   86   79

361   427   542   300   400   477   500   40

2 Choose four of your calculations and use addition to check the answers.

Challenge 3

1 Make up twelve subtraction calculations using these numbers.

7   8   9   97   60   70   80   76   83

700   92   657   685   861   816   953   500   600

2 Choose two different calculations that you can do mentally. Explain what happens in your head when you work them out.

3 Choose four of your calculations and use addition to check the answers.

Sports shop spending

- Add and subtract amounts of money
- Solve word problems involving money and reason mathematically

Work out these money problems. Show your working out. Marcia has €100, Oliver has €200 and Laura has €500.

Challenge 1

a Marcia buys a tennis racquet. How much change will she get?

b Oliver buys a tennis racquet and some trainers. How much does he spend?

c Laura needs a tennis racquet for herself and one for her sister. How much money does she need?

d Laura buys a cricket bat and a scooter. How much does she need to pay?

Challenge 2

a Oliver buys a tennis racquet and some trainers. How much does he spend?

b Laura buys a skateboard. How much change will she get?

c Oliver buys the cheapest item in the shop. How much change will he get?

d Oliver wants two cricket bats. How much more money will he need?

Challenge 3

a Laura buys a skateboard and a helmet. The cost comes to €479. What was the price of the helmet?

b If Oliver and Laura put their money together and bought a skateboard and a scooter, how much change would they get?

c Oliver buys a tennis racquet and some tennis shoes. He spends €128. What was the cost of the tennis shoes?

d Imagine you have €500 to spend. Which items would you buy?

Tally charts

Interpret and present data using tables and charts

Challenge 1

1 George made a table for the types of vehicles passing his school at lunchtime. Copy and complete the table.

Vehicle	Number	Total
car	IIIIIIIIIIIII	
bus	IIIIIIIIIII	
bicycle	IIIIIIIII	
lorry or van	IIIIIIIIII	
motorbike	IIIIIII	

2 a Copy and complete the tally chart below. Use the totals that George found in Question 1. Draw the tally marks and write the totals in the Frequency column.

Vehicle	Tally	Frequency
car		
bus		
bicycle		
lorry or van		
motorbike		

Hint

卅 stands for 5

b How many vehicles were two-wheeled? 2

c How many more cars were there than buses? 2

1 Donna asked some people, "Where do you go to buy your fruit and vegetables?" She made a tally chart for their answers.

Location	Tally	Frequency
supermarket	ⵏⵏ ⵏⵏ ⵏⵏ ⵏⵏ |||	
corner shop	ⵏⵏ ⵏⵏ		
market stall	ⵏⵏ ⵏⵏ ||||	
greengrocer	ⵏⵏ ⵏⵏ ||	

a Copy the tally chart. Count the tally marks. Write the totals in the Frequency column.

b Where do most people buy their fruit and vegetables?

c Which is the least popular location?

d How many more people shopped at the supermarket than at the market stall?

e How many people did Donna ask altogether?

1 Donna asked some other people, "What kind of bread do you prefer?"

Bread	Tally	Frequency
white		18
brown		21
crusty		10
bloomer		6
naan		5

a Copy the table and complete the Tally column.

b What is the most popular type of bread?

c How many more people prefer white bread to crusty bread?

2 Write two statements about the information shown in your table.

3 Look at George's chart in Challenge 1. How might the chart be different if he had collected his data at 6:00 a.m.? Give a reason for your answer.

Charity pictograms

Interpret and present data in pictograms
where one picture represents 2 units

You will need:
• squared paper
• ruler

1 Sam collected this money for charity.

Copy this pictogram.
Count each type of coin.
Complete the pictogram.

Coins collected for charity

1c					
2c					
5c					
10c					

Number of coins

Key

● 2 coins
◖ 1 coin

2 Use the information to answer these questions.

a How many 5c coins were collected? 5

b Which is the least common coin? 2

c How many coins were collected altogether? 19

d How many coins are:

  i gold? 6   **ii** bronze? 13

1 Class 3A collected these coins for charity.

a Count each type of coin and write the total in the table.

b Copy and complete the pictogram.

Coin	Number
1c	17
2c	14
5c	19
10c	7

Coins collected for charity

1c	◐	◐	◐	◐	◐	◐	◐	◐	◖	
2c	◐	◐	◐	◐	◐	◐	◐			
5c	◐	◐	◐	◐	◐	◐	◐	◐	◐	◖
10c	◐	◐	◐	◖						

Number of coins

Key

● 2 coins
◖ 1 coin

2 Use the information to answer these questions.

a How many 5c coins were collected? 19

b Which is the least common coin? 10 c

c How many coins were collected altogether? 57

d How many more 2c coins than 10c coins were collected? 7

1 Draw a pictogram to show what Class 3A collected the next week.

Coin	1c	2c	5c	10c	20c
Number	16	12	8	14	7

2 Write two statements about the information displayed in your pictogram.

◉ 7 coins are collected in gold.

◉ Most of the coins are in bronze.

18.3.20

Picnic bar charts

Interpret and present data in bar charts with intervals labelled in multiples of 2

cherries

raisins

biscuits

sandwiches

You will need:
- squared paper
- ruler
- coloured pencils

Challenge 1

1 Count each item of picnic food.
Copy and complete the tally chart.

Item	Tally	Frequency
sandwiches	⦀⦀ ⦀⦀ ⦀⦀ I	16
biscuits	⦀⦀ ⦀⦀ II	12
cherries	⦀⦀ ⦀⦀ ⦀⦀ ⦀⦀	20
raisins	⦀⦀ III	8

2 Copy and complete the bar chart.

3 a What does the tallest bar show? cherries

   b How many more sandwiches 4
   were there than:

   i   biscuits? 4

   ii   packs of raisins? 8

Picnic food

Number of items

20
18
16
14
12
10
8
6
4
2
0

sandwiches   biscuits   cherries   raisins

Item

1 Copy and complete the table for the number of each type of sandwich.

salad

tuna

chicken

egg

cheese

Sandwich	Frequency
salad	13
tuna	18
egg	10
cheese	16
chicken	12

2 Copy and complete the bar chart.

3 Which sandwich was:

  a the most popular? *tuna*

  b the least popular? *egg*

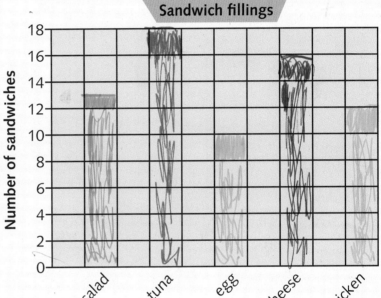

Sandwich fillings

Number of sandwiches

Type of sandwich

4 How many more tuna sandwiches were made than:

  a salad? 5   **b** cheese? 2   **c** chicken? 6   **d** egg? 8

Janice asked 50 children how they liked their eggs prepared.

  a Use this information to make a bar chart and a pictogram of her results.

  b Write three statements describing her results.

Eggs	Frequency
boiled	8
fried	14
poached	17
scrambled	11

41

19.03.2020

Pictograms and bar charts

Use information presented in scaled pictograms, bar charts and tables to answer questions

The pictogram shows the number of bottles of sunscreen sold by Busy Chemists in one week.

You will need:
• squared paper
• ruler
• coloured pencils

Sales of sunscreen

Number of bottles

Mon | Tues | Wed | Thurs | Fri | Sat | Sun

Days of the week

Key

🧴 2 bottles
🧴 1 bottle

1 Copy the table. Write the number of bottles that were sold each day.

2 a Which day had the fewest sales? Tuesday

   b Which two days had the same number of sales?
      Wensday and Sunday

   c How many more bottles were sold on Friday than on Monday? 10 more

Day	Number
Monday	3
Tuesday	2
Wednesday	4
Thursday	6
Friday	13
Saturday	8
Sunday	4

3 Why do you think that Friday had the most sales of sunscreen?

Maybe the Sun is shining on Friday,

The pictogram shows how often the website holidays4u.com was visited in one week.

Website visits

Day of the week							
Sun	❋	❋	❋	❋	❋	❋	❋
Mon	❋	❋	❋	*			
Tues	❋	❋	❋				
Wed	*						
Thurs	❋	❋	❋	❋			
Fri	❋	❋					
Sat	❋	❋	❋	❋	❋	*	

Number of visits

Key

❋ 2 visits

* 1 visit

1 Draw a table to show the number of times the website was visited each day.

2 a How many visits altogether did the website get? *51*

   b Which day had the fewest visits? *Wednsday*

   c On which days were there more than seven visits to the website?
      Sunday Thursday, Saturday

   d How many more visits were made on Saturday than on Monday?
      4 more

1 Draw a bar chart for the data in the 'Website visits' pictogram.

2 How many fewer visits were made on Friday than on Sunday? *10* *fewer*

3 Which two days had the most visits? Explain why you think this is the case. *Sat + Sun*
   beause it is weekend

4 Write two statements about the information in your bar chart.

① *On Wednsday they just got 1 Visit*

② *alltoogether they got 51*

Counting in steps of 50 and 100

- Count on and back in multiples of 50 and 100
- Find 100 more or less than a number

Challenge 1

Write the missing numbers in each row.

a	55	60		70							
b	110			140					190		
c	50				250					500	
d	100						700			1000	

Challenge 2

Find the number of the spaceship by following the footprints. Start on 0 and be careful of the craters!

Challenge 3

1 Choose a start number from the stars. Count forwards from your start number in steps of 100. Continue the count for 6 numbers. Repeat for each start number on the stars.

2 Choose a start number from the moon rocks. Count backwards from your start number in steps of 100. Continue the count for 6 numbers. Repeat for each start number on the moon rocks.

Revising multiplication facts

Consolidate recall of the multiplication facts for the 2, 3, 4, 5, 8 and 10 multiplication tables, and related facts involving multiples of 10

 Challenge 1

Write a multiplication fact for each number coming out of the machine.

a
6
3
7
4
9
×4

b
9
5
8
3
6
×3

c
5
6
9
4
7
×8

 Challenge 2

Find the missing digit, or digits, in each calculation.

a   3 × 9 = 2☆

b   4 × ☆ = 28

c   ☆ × 8 = 32

d   ☆ × 4 = 16

e   7 × 5 = ☆5

f   6 × ☆ = 24

g   8 × 8 = ☆4

h   6 × ☆ = ☆8

i   1☆ × ☆ = 48

j   9 × ☆ = 4☆

k   ☆ × 8 = 6☆

l   9 × ☆ = 3☆

Challenge 3

1 Follow the rules to calculate the score for each dart thrown.

Dart rules:
white: × 80
yellow: × 30
green: × 40

a

b

c

2 For each dartboard, add together the four darts to find the total score. Which dartboard scored the most points?

Revising division facts

Consolidate recall of the division facts for the 2, 3, 4, 5, 8 and 10 multiplication tables, and related facts involving multiples of 10

Challenge 1

Write a division fact for each number coming out of the machine.

a   36
    12
    27
    24
    9

÷3

b   24
    56
    48
    32
    16

÷8

c   12
    36
    20
    44
    32

÷4

Challenge 2

Look at the number sentences on either side of the boxes.
Use these symbols <, = or > to make the number sentences true.

a $45 \div 5$ ☐ $36 \div 3$ b $64 \div 8$ ☐ $32 \div 4$ c $48 \div 8$ ☐ $36 \div 4$

d $56 \div 8$ ☐ $48 \div 4$ e $18 \div 3$ ☐ $28 \div 4$ f $50 \div 10$ ☐ $80 \div 8$

Challenge 3

1 Find the missing digit, or digits, in each calculation.

a $36 \div 9 = \bigcirc$ b $48 \div \triangle = 12$ c $\square \div 4 = 9$

d $21 \div 3 = \blacksquare$ e $\bigcirc 4 \div 8 = 8$ f $\blacktriangle 6 \div \bullet = 2$

g $2\bigcirc \div \blacktriangle = 5$ h $6\triangle \div \blacksquare = 12$ i $3\square \div 8 = \bigcirc$

2 a $360 \div 4 = \bigcirc$ b $280 \div 4 = \blacksquare$ c $\bullet \div 3 = 90$

   d $210 \div 3 = \square$ e $320 \div 8 = \triangle$ f $160 \div \square = 40$

   g $240 \div \blacktriangle = 30$ h $640 \div \bigcirc = 80$ i $350 \div \triangle = 70$

Solving problems

Solve problems and reason mathematically

Challenge
1

Write a multiplication and division fact for each of these pictures.

Example

24

$24 \div 3 = 8$

$8 \times 3 = 24$

a 16

b 20

c 25

d 21

Challenge
2

Read the clues to find the numbers.

a It is twelve times larger than 4.	**b** It is double 8 and 4 more. *20*	**c** It is 20 times larger than 3 multiplied by 2. *120*
d It is double 8 add double 8. *32*	**e** It is 5 less than 25 divided by 5. *0*	**f** It is 5 times more than 9. *45*
g It is half of 64 and half again. *16*	**h** It is the sum of 40 divided by 8 and 24 divided by 4.	**i** It is the same as 9 multiplied by 4 and 3 multiplied by 12. *36 + 36 = 72*

Challenge
3

a Nabil has 64 stamps. Amal has 8 stamps. How many times more stamps does Nabil have than Amal?

b 56 cars are in the car park in the morning. Half are gone by lunchtime. How many are left?

c A pizza is split into slices and eaten. Johan eats 8 slices of pizza and May eats 12 slices of pizza. How many slices in the whole pizza?

d The cook has 40 biscuits. He needs 8 times more for the packed lunches. How many biscuits does he need in total?

e 27 cakes are shared between 9 children. How many for each child? If cakes cost 40c each, how much did each child pay?

Pizza puzzle

Compare and order fractions with the same denominator

 Challenge 1

1 Choose different toppings. Using pizzas that are divided into quarters, how many different combinations can you create? Remember you can only use one topping per slice!

2 For each pizza, write the fraction for one of the toppings.

 Challenge 2

1 Choose different toppings. Using pizzas that are divided into eighths, how many different combinations can you create? Remember you can only use one topping per slice!

2 For each pizza, write the fraction for one of the toppings.

 Challenge 3

1 Choose different ingredients. Using pizzas that are divided into tenths, how many different combinations can you create? Remember you can only use one topping per slice!

2 For each pizza, write the fraction for one of the toppings.

3 Write a fraction addition for each pizza.

Example

$$\frac{4}{10} + \frac{6}{10} = 1$$

Subtracting fractions

Subtract fractions within one whole

You will need:
- interlocking cubes of 2 different colours
- coloured pencils

 1 Make a rod using 6 cubes in two different colours. Put cubes of the same colour together.

    a Draw it in your book.

    b Write a fraction subtraction to show the answer when the cubes of one colour are removed from the whole rod.

    c Repeat the above twice more with different numbers of each colour.

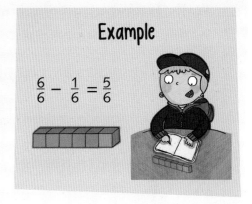

Example

$$\frac{6}{6} - \frac{1}{6} = \frac{5}{6}$$

2 Make one more rod using 5 cubes. Put cubes of the same colour together. Draw it in your book. Write a fraction subtraction to show the answer when the cubes of one colour are removed from the whole rod.

 1 Look at these rods. Write a fraction subtraction to show the answer when the cubes of one colour are removed from the whole rod.

    a   **b**   **c**

    d   **e**   **f**

2 Draw three rods of your own and colour each one in two colours. Write a fraction subtraction to show the answer when the cubes of one colour are removed from the whole rod.

1 a $\frac{4}{4} - \frac{1}{4} =$ **b** $\frac{5}{5} - \frac{4}{5} =$ **c** $\frac{6}{6} - \frac{2}{6} =$ **d** $\frac{8}{8} - \frac{3}{8} =$ **e** $\frac{10}{10} - \frac{3}{10} =$

2 Explain why $\frac{8}{8}$ is the same as one whole.

3 a $\frac{3}{3} - \boxed{} = \frac{1}{3}$ **b** $\frac{5}{5} - \boxed{} = \frac{3}{5}$ **c** $\frac{6}{6} - \boxed{} = \frac{5}{6}$ **d** $\frac{8}{8} - \boxed{} = \frac{6}{8}$

Equivalent fractions

Recognise equivalent fractions

You will need:
- interlocking cubes of two different colours
- coloured pencils

Challenge 1

Using cubes, make some snakes that can join the Half-Snake Club. They need to be half one colour and half another colour.

Draw the snakes and complete this sentence for each snake:

$\frac{1}{2}$ of my snake is ▢ and $\frac{1}{2}$ of my snake is ▢.

See how many different snakes you can make.

Half-Snake Club

Challenge 2

Using cubes, make some snakes that can join the Half-Snake Club.

Draw the snakes and write the fraction that is equivalent to half for each one.

Make 10 different snakes.

Example

$\frac{1}{2} = \frac{2}{4}$

Challenge 3

1 What does 'equivalent' mean?

2 Draw some snakes, and write the fractions, that are equivalent to one-quarter.

I'm $\frac{1}{4}$ yellow, so I can join the One-quarter Snake Club.

Example

$\frac{1}{4} = \frac{2}{8}$

Fractions wall

Recognise equivalent fractions

You will need:
• three equal strips of paper

1 Fold three strips of paper to make a fraction wall.

   a Fold one strip in half.

   b Fold another strip to show quarters.

   c Fold the remaining strip to show eighths.

2 Stick them into your book, making sure the middle folds all line up.

3 What fractions can you see that are the same? Record the fractions. like this: $\frac{1}{2} = \frac{2}{4}$.

1 Fold five strips of paper to make a fraction wall. Make halves, quarters, sixths, eighths and tenths.

2 Stick them into your book, making sure the middle folds all line up.

3 What fractions can you see that are the same? Record them like this: $\frac{1}{4} = \frac{2}{8}$.

You will need:
• five equal strips of paper

I can see that $\frac{1}{2}$ and $\frac{2}{4}$ are the same.

1 Fold seven strips of paper to make a fraction wall. Make halves, thirds, quarters, sixths, eighths, tenths and twelfths.

You will need:
• seven equal strips of paper

   a What fractions can you see that are the same? Record them like this: $\frac{1}{3} = \frac{2}{6}$.

   b Which fraction strips were the hardest to fold? Explain why.

Perimeters of rectangles

Calculate the perimeter of rectangles in centimetres and metres

Example

perimeter = 3 cm + 2 cm + 3 cm + 2 cm = 10 cm

Challenge 1

Find the perimeter of each rectangle in centimetres.

a

b

Challenge 2

1 The dots are 1 cm apart. Find the perimeter of each rectangle in centimetres.

a

b

c

2 Write the perimeter of each vegetable bed in metres.

Challenge 3

Monty needs more space to grow salads and potatoes. He joins vegetable beds A and E in Challenge 2 to make one bed for salads, and beds B and D for potatoes. Find the perimeter of:

a the new bed for salads   **b** the new bed for potatoes

Drawing and calculating perimeters

Using a ruler, draw and calculate the perimeter of rectangles

On 1 cm squared paper draw different rectangles with perimeters of:

a   10 cm   b   14 cm

c   18 cm

Example

perimeter = 12 cm

You will need:
• ruler
• 1 cm squared paper

On 1 cm square dot grid paper draw a square then all the rectangles that have a perimeter of:

a   4 cm   b   8 cm

c   12 cm   d   16 cm

e   20 cm

Example

perimeter = 14 cm

You will need:
• ruler
• 1 cm square dot grid paper

Do Challenge 2 then copy and complete the table.

You will need:
• ruler
• 1 cm square dot grid paper

Side of square	Perimeter of square	Number of rectangles with same perimeter	Total number of squares and rectangles
1 cm	4 cm	0	1
2 cm	8 cm		
3 cm			
4 cm			
5 cm			

Regular perimeters

Measure and calculate the perimeter of 2-D shapes

You will need:
• ruler

Challenge 1

Use your ruler to measure the perimeter of these regular shapes in centimetres.

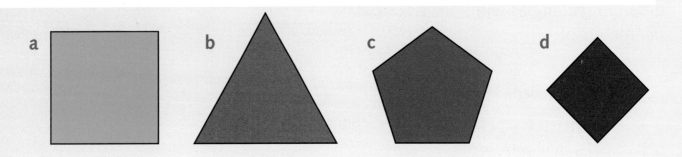

a   b   c   d

Challenge 2

Use your ruler to measure the perimeter of these regular shapes in centimetres.

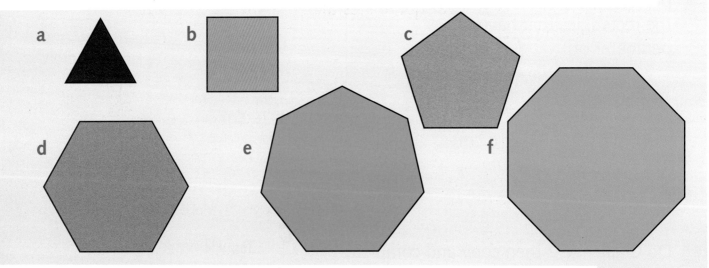

a   b   c   d   e   f

Challenge 3

1 Copy and complete the table for the regular shapes in Challenge 2.

Number of sides of shape	3	4	5	6	7	8
Perimeter in centimetres						

2 If you continue the pattern, what will the perimeter of these regular shapes measure?

   a   10 sides   b   12 sides

Perimeters of 2-D shapes

Measure and calculate the perimeter of 2-D shapes

You will need:
- four to five square tiles
- 1 cm squared paper
- ruler
- coloured pencils

Challenge 1

1 Make each shape with four square tiles then draw the shape on to 1 cm squared paper.

 a   b   c   d

2 Below each shape, write its perimeter.

Challenge 2

1 Make each shape with five square tiles then draw the shape on to 1 cm squared paper.

a   b   c   d

e   f   g

2 Below each shape, write its perimeter.

Challenge 3

With five squares, you can make 12 different shapes. Seven of the shapes are drawn in Challenge 2.

1 Find the remaining five shapes.

2 Draw them on to 1 cm squared paper and calculate their perimeters.

Maths facts

Problem solving

The seven steps to solving word problems
1 Read the problem carefully.   **2** What do you have to find?
3 What facts are given?   **4** Which of the facts do you need?   **5** Make a plan.
6 Carry out your plan to obtain your answer.   **7** Check your answer.

Number and place value

100	200	300	400	500	600	700	800	900
10	20	30	40	50	60	70	80	90
1	2	3	4	5	6	7	8	9

Addition and subtraction

Number facts

+	0	1	2	3	4	5	6	7	8	9	10
0	0	1	2	3	4	5	6	7	8	9	10
1	1	2	3	4	5	6	7	8	9	10	11
2	2	3	4	5	6	7	8	9	10	11	12
3	3	4	5	6	7	8	9	10	11	12	13
4	4	5	6	7	8	9	10	11	12	13	14
5	5	6	7	8	9	10	11	12	13	14	15
6	6	7	8	9	10	11	12	13	14	15	16
7	7	8	9	10	11	12	13	14	15	16	17
8	8	9	10	11	12	13	14	15	16	17	18
9	9	10	11	12	13	14	15	16	17	18	19
10	10	11	12	13	14	15	16	17	18	19	20

+	11	12	13	14	15	16	17	18	19	20
0	11	12	13	14	15	16	17	18	19	20
1	12	13	14	15	16	17	18	19	20	
2	13	14	15	16	17	18	19	20		
3	14	15	16	17	18	19	20			
4	15	16	17	18	19	20				
5	16	17	18	19	20					
6	17	18	19	20						
7	18	19	20							
8	19	20								
9	20									

Number facts

+	0	10	20	30	40	50	60	70	80	90	100
0	0	10	20	30	40	50	60	70	80	90	100
10	10	20	30	40	50	60	70	80	90	100	110
20	20	30	40	50	60	70	80	90	100	110	120
30	30	40	50	60	70	80	90	100	110	120	130
40	40	50	60	70	80	90	100	110	120	130	140
50	50	60	70	80	90	100	110	120	130	140	150
60	60	70	80	90	100	110	120	130	140	150	160
70	70	80	90	100	110	120	130	140	150	160	170
80	80	90	100	110	120	130	140	150	160	170	180
90	90	100	110	120	130	140	150	160	170	180	190
100	100	110	120	130	140	150	160	170	180	190	200

+	110	120	130	140	150	160	170	180	190	200
0	110	120	130	140	150	160	170	180	190	200
10	120	130	140	150	160	170	180	190	200	210
20	130	140	150	160	170	180	190	200	210	220
30	140	150	160	170	180	190	200	210	220	230
40	150	160	170	180	190	200	210	220	230	240
50	160	170	180	190	200	210	220	230	240	250
60	170	180	190	200	210	220	230	240	250	260
70	180	190	200	210	220	230	240	250	260	270
80	190	200	210	220	230	240	250	260	270	280
90	200	210	220	230	240	250	260	270	280	290
100	210	220	230	240	250	260	270	280	290	300

Written methods – addition

Example: 548 + 387

Expanded written method

```
    5 4 8
  + 3 8 7
      1 5
    1 2 0
    8 0 0
    9 3 5
```

Formal written method

```
    5 4 8
  + 3 8 7
    9 3 5
    1 1
```

Written methods – subtraction

Example: 582 – 237

Formal written method

```
      7 12
    5 8 2
  - 2 3 7
    3 4 5
```

Multiplication and division

Number facts

x	2	3	4	5	8	10
1	2	3	4	5	8	10
2	4	6	8	10	16	20
3	6	9	12	15	24	30
4	8	12	16	20	32	40
5	10	15	20	25	40	50
6	12	18	24	30	48	60
7	14	21	28	35	56	70
8	16	24	32	40	64	80
9	18	27	36	45	72	90
10	20	30	40	50	80	100
11	22	33	44	55	88	110
12	24	36	48	60	96	120

Written methods – division

Example: $92 \div 4$

Partitioning

$$92 \div 4 = (80 \div 4) + (12 \div 4)$$
$$= 20 + 3$$
$$= 23$$

Expanded written method

```
      2 3
  4 ) 9 2
      8 0    20 × 4
      1 2
      1 2    3 × 4
          0
```

Formal written method

```
      2 3
  4 ) 9 ¹2
```

Written methods – multiplication

Example: 63×8

Partitioning

$$63 \times 8 = (60 \times 8) + (3 \times 8)$$
$$= 480 + 24$$
$$= 504$$

Grid method

×	60	3	
8	480	24	= 504

Expanded written method

```
      6 3
  ×     8
      2 4    ( 3 × 8)
    4 8 0    (60 × 8)
    5 0 4
      1
```

Formal written method

```
      6 3
  ×   ₂8
    5 0 4
```

Fractions

$\frac{1}{2}$	
$\frac{1}{4}$	
$\frac{1}{8}$	
$\frac{1}{3}$	
$\frac{1}{6}$	
$\frac{1}{9}$	
$\frac{1}{12}$	
$\frac{1}{5}$	
$\frac{1}{10}$	

Measurement

Length
1 metre (m) = 100 centimetres (cm) = 1000 millimetres (mm)

Mass
1 kilogram (kg) = 1000 grams (g)

Capacity
1 litre (*l*) = 1000 millilitres (ml)

Time

1 year	=	12 months
	=	365 days
	=	366 days (leap year)
1 week	=	7 days
1 day	=	24 hours
1 hour	=	60 minutes
1 minute	=	60 seconds

12-hour clock 24-hour clock

Properties of shape

right-angled triangle equilateral triangle isosceles triangle scalene triangle

        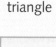

circle semi-circle pentagon hexagon heptagon octagon square rectangle

cube cuboid cone cylinder sphere triangular prism triangular-based pyramid (tetrahedron) square-based pyramid

59